LIFE
Lessons

WITH MAX LUCADO

BOOK OF
2 CORINTHIANS

REMEMBERING WHAT MATTERS

MAX LUCADO

Prepared by
THE LIVINGSTONE CORPORATION

Published by
THOMAS NELSON™
Since 1798

www.thomasnelson.com

Life Lessons with Max Lucado—Book of 2 Corinthians

Copyright © by Thomas Nelson, 2007

Published in Nashville, Tennessee. Thomas Nelson is a trademark of Thomas Nelson, Inc.

Thomas Nelson, Inc. titles may be purchased in bulk for educational, business, fundraising, or sales promotional use. For information, please email SpecialMarkets@ThomasNelson.com.

Scipture passages taken from:
J. B. Phillips: The New Testament in Modern English, Revised Edition (PHILLIPS). Copyright © J. B. Phillips 1958, 1960, 1972. Used by permission of Macmillan Publishing Co., Inc.
The Holy Bible, New Century Version (NCV). Copyright ©1987, 1988, 1991 by Word Publishing. All rights reserved.
The New English Bible (NEB). Copyright © 1961, 1970 by the delegates of the Oxford University Press and the Syndics of the Cambridge University Press. Reprinted by permission.
The HOLY BIBLE, NEW INTERNATIONAL VERSION® (NIV). Copyright © 1973, 1978, 1984 by International Bible Society. Used by permission of Zondervan Publishing House. All rights reserved. The "NIV" and "New International Version" trademarks are registered in the United States Patent and Trademark Office by International Bible Society. Use of either trademark requires the permission of International Bible Society.
The Holy Bible, New King James Version (NKJV). Copyright © 1979, 1980, 1982 by Thomas Nelson. All rights reserved.
THE MESSAGE (MSG). Copyright © 1993, 1994, 1995, 1996, 2000, 2001, 2002. Used by permission of NavPress Publishing Group.

Material for the "Inspiration" sections taken from the following books:
Come Thirsty. Copyright © 2004 by Max Lucado. W Publishing Group, a Division of Thomas Nelson, Inc., Nashville, Tennessee.
Cure for the Common Life. Copyright © 2005 by Max Lucado. W Publishing Group, a Division of Thomas Nelson, Inc., Nashville, Tennessee.
A Gentle Thunder. Copyright © 1995 by Max Lucado. W Publishing Group, a Division of Thomas Nelson, Inc., Nashville, Tennessee.
In the Grip of Grace. Copyright © 1996 by Max Lucado. W Publishing Group, a Division of Thomas Nelson, Inc., Nashville, Tennessee.
It's Not About Me. Copyright © 2004 by Max Lucado. Integrity Publishers, Brentwood, Tennessee.
Just Like Jesus. Copyright © 1998 by Max Lucado. W Publishing Group, a Division of Thomas Nelson, Inc., Nashville, Tennessee.
Traveling Light. Copyright © 2001 by Max Lucado. W Publishing Group, a Division of Thomas Nelson, Inc., Nashville, Tennessee.
When Christ Comes Copyright © 1999 by Max Lucado. W Publishing Group, a Division of Thomas Nelson, Inc., Nashville, Tennessee.
When God Whispers Your Name. Copyright © 1994, 1999 by Max Lucado. W Publishing Group, a Division of Thomas Nelson, Inc., Nashville, Tennessee.

Produced with the assistance of the Livingstone Corporation. Project staff include Jake Barton, Joel Bartlett, Andy Culbertson, Mary Horner Collins, Will Reaves, and Rachel Hawkins.
Editor: Len Woods
Cover Art and Interior Design by Kirk Luttrell of the Livingstone Corporation
Interior Composition by Rachel Hawkins of the Livingstone Corporation

ISBN-10: 1-4185-0972-8
ISBN-13: 978-1-4185-0972-9

Printed in the United States of America.
10 11 WC 9 8 7 6 5

WITH MAX LUCADO

CONTENTS

HOW TO STUDY THE BIBLE

This is a peculiar book you are holding. Words crafted in another language. Deeds done in a distant era. Events recorded in a far-off land. Counsel offered to a foreign people. This is a peculiar book.

It's surprising that anyone reads it. It's too old. Some of its writings date back five thousand years. It's too bizarre. The book speaks of incredible floods, fires, earthquakes, and people with supernatural abilities. It's too radical. The Bible calls for undying devotion to a carpenter who called himself God's Son.

Logic says this book shouldn't survive. Too old, too bizarre, too radical.

The Bible has been banned, burned, scoffed, and ridiculed. Scholars have mocked it as foolish. Kings have branded it as illegal. A thousand times over, the grave has been dug and the dirge has begun, but somehow the Bible never stays in the grave. Not only has it survived; it has thrived. It is the single most popular book in all of history. It has been the best-selling book in the world for years!

There is no way on earth to explain it. Which perhaps is the only explanation. The answer? The Bible's durability is not found on earth; it is found in heaven. For the millions who have tested its claims and claimed its promises, there is but one answer: the Bible is God's book and God's voice.

As you read it, you would be wise to give some thought to two questions. What is the purpose of the Bible? and How do I study the Bible? Time spent reflecting on these two issues will greatly enhance your Bible study.

What is the purpose of the Bible?

Let the Bible itself answer that question.

Since you were a child you have known the Holy Scriptures which are able to make you wise. And that wisdom leads to salvation through faith in Christ Jesus. (2 Tim. 3:15 NCV)

The purpose of the Bible? Salvation. God's highest passion is to get his children home. His book, the Bible, describes his plan of salvation. The purpose of the Bible is to proclaim God's plan and passion to save his children.

That is the reason this book has endured through the centuries. It dares to tackle the toughest questions about life: Where do I go after I die? Is there a God? What do I do with my fears? The Bible offers answers to these crucial questions. It is the treasure map that leads us to God's highest treasure, eternal life.

But how do we use the Bible? Countless copies of Scripture sit unread on book-shelves and nightstands simply because people don't know how to read it. What can we do to make the Bible real in our lives?

The clearest answer is found in the words of Jesus. He promised:

Ask, and God will give to you. Search, and you will find. Knock, and the door will open for you. (Matt. 7:7 NCV)

The first step in understanding the Bible is asking God to help us. We should read prayerfully. If anyone understands God's Word, it is because of God and not the reader.

But the Helper will teach you everything and will cause you to remember all that I told you. The Helper is the Holy Spirit whom the Father will send in my name. (John 14:26 NCV)

Before reading the Bible, pray. Invite God to speak to you. Don't go to Scripture looking for your idea; go searching for his.

Not only should we read the Bible prayerfully; we should read it carefully. *Search and you will find* is the pledge. The Bible is not a newspaper to be skimmed but rather a mine to be quarried.

Search for it like silver, and hunt for it like hidden treasure. Then you will understand respect for the LORD, and you will find that you know God. (Prov. 2:4–5 NCV)

Any worthy find requires effort. The Bible is no exception. To understand the Bible you don't have to be brilliant, but you must be willing to roll up your sleeves and search.

Be a worker who is not ashamed and who uses the true teaching in the right way. (2 Tim. 2:15 NCV)

Here's a practical point. Study the Bible a bit at a time. Hunger is not satisfied by eating twenty-one meals in one sitting once a week. The body needs a steady diet to remain strong. So does the soul. When God sent food to his people in the wilderness, he didn't provide loaves already made. Instead, he sent them manna in the shape of *"thin flakes like frost . . . on the desert ground"* (Ex. 16:14 NCV).

God gave manna in limited portions. God sends spiritual food the same way. He opens the heavens with just enough nutrients for today's hunger. He provides *"a command here, a command there. A rule here, a rule there. A little lesson here, a little lesson there"* (Isa. 28:10 NCV).

Don't be discouraged if your reading reaps a small harvest. Some days a lesser portion is all that is needed. What is important is to search every day for that day's message. A steady diet of God's Word over a lifetime builds a healthy soul and mind.

A little girl returned from her first day at school. Her mom asked, "Did you learn anything?"

"Apparently not enough," the girl responded, "I have to go back tomorrow and the next day and the next . . ."

Such is the case with learning. And such is the case with Bible study. Understanding comes little by little over a lifetime.

There is a third step in understanding the Bible. After the asking and seeking comes the knocking. After you ask and search, then knock.

Knock, and the door will open for you. (Matt. 7:7 NCV)

To knock is to stand at God's door. To make yourself available. To climb the steps, cross the porch, stand at the doorway, and volunteer. Knocking goes beyond the realm of thinking and into the realm of acting.

To knock is to ask, What can I do? How can I obey? Where can I go?

It's one thing to know what to do. It's another to do it. But for those who do it, those who choose to obey, a special reward awaits them.

The truly happy are those who carefully study God's perfect law that makes people free, and they continue to study it. They do not forget what they heard, but they obey what God's teaching says. Those who do this will be made happy. (James 1:25 NCV)

What a promise. Happiness comes to those who do what they read! It's the same with medicine. If you only read the label but ignore the pills, it won't help. It's the same with food. If you only read the recipe but never cook, you won't be fed. And it's the same with the Bible. If you only read the words but never obey, you'll never know the joy God has promised.

Ask. Search. Knock. Simple, isn't it? Why don't you give it a try? If you do, you'll see why you are holding the most remarkable book in history.

INTRODUCTION TO THE BOOK OF 2 CORINTHIANS

At a school in a small village, there was one girl who came early. She helped the teacher prepare the room for the day. The same girl would stay late—cleaning the board and dusting the erasers. During class she was attentive. She sat close to the teacher, absorbing the lessons.

One day when the other children were unruly and inattentive, the teacher used the girl as an example. "Why can't you be like her? She listens. She works. She comes early. She stays late."

"It isn't fair to ask us to be like her," a boy blurted out from the rear of the room.

"Why?" asked the teacher.

The boy was uncomfortable, wishing he hadn't spoken. "She has an advantage," he shrugged. "She is an orphan," he almost whispered.

The boy was right. The girl had an advantage. An advantage of knowing that school, as tedious as it was, was better than the orphanage. Since she knew that, she appreciated what the others took for granted.

We, too, were orphans.

Alone.

No name. No future. No hope.

Were it not for our adoption as his children, we would have no place to belong. We sometimes forget that.

The Corinthians forgot.

They had grown puffy in their achievements and divisive in their fellowship. They argued over the correct leader, the greater gifts. They rebelled against Paul's leadership. They were indifferent to sin and insensitive in worship.

Paul defends his ministry and admonishes the Christians to remember to whom they belong. "Look closely at yourselves," Paul says (13:5 NCV). Paul's words are clear. "If anyone belongs to Christ, there is a new creation. The old things have gone; everything is made new!" (5:17).

Good reminder.

Not just for them but for us as well. For if we forget, we, too, will be like the students who did just enough to pass the grade and never enough to show their thanks.

LESSON ONE

SUFFERING

MAX
LUCADO

REFLECTION

Life is full of ups and downs. We can be cruising along, everything working perfectly. Then, suddenly, unexpectedly, the wheels can go flying off, and
we find ourselves in the proverbial ditch, wondering, "What just happened?"
Which end of the spectrum best describes your life just now?

SITUATION

Less than a year after writing 1 Corinthians, Paul wrote this epistle. Unforeseen
circumstances had forced Paul to delay a planned visit to Corinth. This change
in plans gave certain false teachers in Corinth ammunition to accuse him of
being unreliable and not a true apostle—charges that deeply grieved Paul and
caused many to question his motives. Paul found comfort in God.

OBSERVATION

Read 2 Corinthians 1:1–11 from the NCV or the NKJV.

NCV

¹*From Paul, an apostle of Christ Jesus. I am an apostle because that is what God wanted. Also from Timothy our brother in Christ.*

To the church of God in Corinth, and to all of God's people everywhere in Southern Greece:

²*Grace and peace to you from God our Father and the Lord Jesus Christ.*

³*Praise be to the God and Father of our Lord Jesus Christ. God is the Father who is full of mercy and all comfort.* ⁴*He comforts us every time we have trouble, so when others have trouble, we can comfort them with the same comfort God gives us.* ⁵*We share in the many sufferings of Christ. In the same way, much comfort comes to us through Christ.* ⁶*If we have troubles, it is for your comfort and salvation, and if we have comfort, you also have comfort. This helps you to accept patiently the same sufferings we have.* ⁷*Our hope for you is strong, knowing that you share in our sufferings and also in the comfort we receive.*

⁸*Brothers and sisters, we want you to know about the trouble we suffered in Asia. We had great burdens there that were beyond our own strength. We even gave up hope of living.* ⁹*Truly, in our own hearts we believed we would die. But this happened so we would not trust in ourselves but in God, who raises people from the dead.* ¹⁰*God saved us from these great dangers of death, and he will continue to save us. We have put our hope in him, and he will save us again.* ¹¹*And you can help us with your prayers. Then many people will give thanks for us—that God blessed us because of their many prayers.*

NKJV

¹*Paul, an apostle of Jesus Christ by the will of God, and Timothy our brother,*

To the church of God which is at Corinth, with all the saints who are in all Achaia:

²*Grace to you and peace from God our Father and the Lord Jesus Christ.*

³*Blessed be the God and Father of our Lord Jesus Christ, the Father of mercies and God of all comfort,* ⁴*who comforts us in all our tribulation, that we may be able to comfort those who are in any trouble, with the comfort with which we ourselves are comforted by God.* ⁵*For as the sufferings of Christ abound in us, so our consolation also abounds through Christ.* ⁶*Now if we are afflicted, it is for your consolation and salvation, which is effective for enduring the same sufferings which we also suffer. Or if we are comforted, it is for your consolation and salvation.* ⁷*And our hope for you is steadfast, because we know that as you are partakers of the sufferings, so also you will partake of the consolation.*

8For we do not want you to be ignorant, brethren, of our trouble which came to us in Asia: that we were burdened beyond measure, above strength, so that we despaired even of life. 9Yes, we had the sentence of death in ourselves, that we should not trust in ourselves but in God who raises the dead, 10who delivered us from so great a death, and does deliver us; in whom we trust that He will still deliver us, 11you also helping together in prayer for us, that thanks may be given by many persons on our behalf for the gift granted to us through many.

EXPLORATION

1. How do Paul's letters differ from the letters and e-mails you write?

2. How does Paul describe God?

3. How would you explain the difference between hope and comfort?

4. Paul gives us a window into his emotional state during the worst of his recent trials. What words and phrases does he use?

5. According to Paul, what are some of the positive things that can result when we look to God during life's trials?

INSPIRATION

"That evening Jesus' followers went down to Lake Galilee. It was dark now, and Jesus had not yet come to them. The followers got into a boat and started across the lake to Capernaum. By now a strong wind was blowing, and the waves on the lake were getting bigger" (John 6:16–18 NCV) . . .

They did exactly what Jesus said, and look what it got them! A night on a storm-tossed sea with their Master somewhere on the shore.

It's one thing to suffer for doing wrong. Something else entirely to suffer for doing right. But it happens. And when the storm bursts, it washes away the naive assumption that if I do right, I will never suffer.

Just ask the faithful couple whose crib is empty and whose womb is barren.

Just ask the businessman whose honest work was rewarded with runaway inflation.

Just ask the student who took a stand for the truth and got mocked . . . the husband who took a chance and forgave his wife, only to be betrayed again.

And so the winds blow.

And so the boat bounces.

And so the disciples wonder, "Why the storm, and where is Jesus?" . . .

Mark tells us that during the storm Jesus "saw his followers struggling" (Mark 6:48). Through the night he saw them. Through the storm he saw them. And like a loving father he waited. He waited until the right time, until the right moment. He waited until he knew it was time to come, and then he came.

What made it the right time? I don't know. Why was the ninth hour better than the fourth or fifth? I can't answer that. Why does God wait until the money is gone? Why does he wait until the sickness has lingered? Why does he choose to wait until the other side of the grave to answer the prayers for healing?

I don't know. I only know his timing is always right. I can only say he will do what is best. "God will always give what is right to his people who cry to him night and day, and he will not be slow to answer them" (Luke 18:7).

Though you hear nothing, he is speaking. Though you see nothing, he is acting. With God there are no accidents. Every incident is intended to bring us closer to him. (From *A Gentle Thunder* by Max Lucado)

REACTION

6. How does the incident of Christ's disciples on a stormy sea (John 6) echo the truths presented in 2 Corinthians 1?

7. Think back over your life to the hardest trials and most excruciating times of suffering. What got you through? Gods Word!

8. What are the primary ways that God brings comfort to his hurting children?

9. Many people in the midst of difficulty become negative and resort to incessant complaining. Not Paul. How do you think he maintained his hopeful outlook?

10. How can a person change his or her attitude in the midst of suffering and use it to grow in faith?

11. Who in your sphere of influence is facing a hard time right now? How can Paul's teaching benefit them?

LIFE LESSONS

A renowned psychiatrist was once asked how to overcome depression. His advice? "Get dressed, lock your house, go find someone who is in need, and serve that person." In other words, get the focus off yourself and look for ways to help others. This others-centered mind-set is to be the hallmark of every Christian's life. Jesus constantly lived to serve others (Matt. 20:28). The apostle Paul did likewise. In a situation where lesser men would have decided to throw a major "pity party," licking their wounds and lamenting their woeful condition, Paul turned to God for comfort. Then he picked up a pen and determined to write a letter that would help the Corinthians think and live in ways that honor God.

DEVOTION

Thank you, God, for being my merciful Father and the source of ultimate comfort. You are so faithful and good! Teach me the holy habit of looking to you to meet all my needs. Show me daily how to draw upon your infinite resources so that I might be a source of compassion to others who hurt.

For more Bible passages on looking to God for comfort in suffering, see Psalm 23:1–4; 119:50–52; John 14:16–17; Philippians 2:1–2; and James 1:3–12.

To complete the book of 2 Corinthians during this twelve-part study, read 2 Corinthians 1:1–11.

JOURNALING

How does your mind-set affect your mood?

L E S S O N   T W O

PLANS

MAX
LUCADO

REFLECTION

Perhaps you've heard the old phrase "The best laid plans of mice and men . . ." People say this when things go awry, when a predetermined agenda falls apart. Describe a recent experience in which your plans (travel or business or financial, etc.) did not work out, resulting in either internal angst or interpersonal friction.

SITUATION

For whatever reasons—internal prompting, external interference, or perhaps a bit of both—Paul did not visit Corinth as he had planned. Some influential leaders in the church used this situation to call into question Paul's credibility as an apostle and to undermine his authority and his message.

OBSERVATION

Read 2 Corinthians 1:12—2:4 from the NCV or the NKJV.

NCV

12This is what we are proud of, and I can say it with a clear conscience: In everything we have done in the world, and especially with you, we have had an honest and sincere heart from God. We did this by God's grace, not by the kind of wisdom the world has. 13-14We write to you only what you can read and understand. And I hope that as you have understood some things about us, you may come to know everything about us. Then you can be proud of us, as we will be proud of you on the day our Lord Jesus Christ comes again.

15I was so sure of all this that I made plans to visit you first so you could be blessed twice. 16I planned to visit you on my way to Macedonia and again on my way back. I wanted to get help from you for my trip to Judea. 17Do you think that I made these plans without really meaning it? Or maybe you think I make plans as the world does, so that I say yes, yes and at the same time no, no.

18But if you can believe God, you can believe that what we tell you is never both yes and no. 19The Son of God, Jesus Christ, that Silas and Timothy and I preached to you, was not yes and no. In Christ it has always been yes. 20The yes to all of God's promises is in Christ, and through Christ we say yes to the glory of God. 21Remember, God is the One who makes you and us strong in Christ. God made us his chosen people. 22He put his mark on us to show that we are his, and he put his Spirit in our hearts to be a guarantee for all he has promised.

23I tell you this, and I ask God to be my witness that this is true: The reason I did not come back to Corinth was to keep you from being punished or hurt. 24We are not trying to control your faith. You are strong in faith. But we are workers with you for your own joy.

2:1So I decided that my next visit to you would not be another one to make you sad. 2If I make you sad, who will make me glad? Only you can make me glad—particularly the person whom I made sad. 3I wrote you a letter for this reason: that when I came to you I would not be made sad by the people who should make me happy. I felt sure of all of you, that you would share my joy. 4When I wrote to you before, I was very troubled and unhappy in my heart, and I wrote with many tears. I did not write to make you sad, but to let you know how much I love you.

NKJV

12For our boasting is this: the testimony of our conscience that we conducted ourselves in the world in simplicity and godly sincerity, not with fleshly wisdom but by the grace of God, and more abundantly toward you. 13For we are not writing any other things to you than what you read or understand. Now I trust you will understand, even to the end 14(as also you have understood us in part), that we are your boast as you also are ours, in the day of the Lord Jesus.

15And in this confidence I intended to come to you before, that you might have a second benefit— 16to pass by way of you to Macedonia, to come again from Macedonia to you, and be helped by you on my way to Judea. 17Therefore, when I was planning this, did I do it lightly? Or the things I plan, do I plan according to the flesh, that with me there should be Yes, Yes, and No, No? 18But as God is faithful, our word to you was not Yes and No. 19For the Son of God, Jesus Christ, who was preached among you by us—by me, Silvanus, and Timothy—was not Yes and No, but in Him was Yes. 20For all the promises of God in Him are Yes, and in Him Amen, to the glory of God through us. 21Now He who establishes us with you in Christ and has anointed us is God, 22who also has sealed us and given us the Spirit in our hearts as a guarantee.

23Moreover I call God as witness against my soul, that to spare you I came no more to Corinth. 24Not that we have dominion over your faith, but are fellow workers for your joy; for by faith you stand.

3:1But I determined this within myself, that I would not come again to you in sorrow. 2For if I make you sorrowful, then who is he who makes me glad but the one who is made sorrowful by me?

3And I wrote this very thing to you, lest, when I came, I should have sorrow over those from whom I ought to have joy, having confidence in you all that my joy is the joy of you all. 4For out of much affliction and anguish of heart I wrote to you, with many tears, not that you should be grieved, but that you might know the love which I have so abundantly for you.

EXPLORATION

1. What event caused the Corinthian church to distrust Paul?

2. What does Paul claim here about his true motives?

3. How does Paul differentiate between his way of planning and the world's way of planning?

4. In this section, Paul mentions each person of the Trinity. What revealing things does he say about each?

5. What are the reasons stated in verses 2:23–3:4 for Paul's change of plans?

INSPIRATION

When David, who was a warrior, minstrel, and ambassador for God, searched for an illustration of God, he remembered his days as a shepherd. He remembered how he lavished attention on the sheep day and night. How he slept with them and watched over them.

And the way he cared for the sheep reminded him of the way God cares for us. David rejoiced to say, "The LORD is my shepherd," and in so doing he proudly implied, "I am his sheep."

Still uncomfortable with being considered a sheep? Will you humor me and take a simple quiz? See if you succeed in self-reliance. Raise your hand if any of the following describe you.

You can control your moods. You're never grumpy or sullen. You can't relate to Jekyll and Hyde. You're always upbeat and upright. Does that describe you? No? Well, let's try another.

You are at peace with everyone. Every relationship as sweet as fudge. Even your old flames speak highly of you. Love all and are loved by all. Is that you? If not, how about this description?

You have no fears. Call you the Teflon toughie. Wall Street plummets—no problem. Heart condition discovered—yawn. World War III starts—what's for dinner?

Does this describe you?

You need no forgiveness. Never made a mistake. As square as a game of checkers. As clean as grandma's kitchen. Never cheated, never lied, never lied about cheating. Is that you? No?

Let's evaluate this. You can't control your moods. A few of your relationships are shaky. You have fears and faults. Hmmm. Do you really want to hang on to your chest of self-reliance? Sounds to me as if you could use a shepherd. (From *Traveling Light* by Max Lucado)

REACTION

6. The "job description" of a sheep is to go wherever the shepherd guides it. Why is it so hard for us as Christians to let go of our agendas and follow Christ?

7. How can we tell if our hearts are "honest and sincere" (v. 12 NCV)?

8. When you sense God leading you in a new and different direction than you had planned, how do you typically respond?

9. How does a Christian develop the ability to follow wherever the Shepherd, the Holy Spirit, is leading? (See Galatians 5:18, 25 for more on being led by the Spirit.)

10. How do you respond when your actions are misunderstood and you are unfairly accused or your character is questioned?

11. Why do you think Paul had such a deep, almost "stubborn" love and relentless concern for a church that caused him so much grief?

LIFE LESSONS

One thing we can count on for sure is the unpredictability of life. If we commit to follow Christ, the Good Shepherd, we should expect the unexpected. Sometimes divinely allowed or orchestrated events will block our path. God's Spirit will suddenly nudge us down a different course. In some situations, our "new" plans or direction may be viewed as foolish by others. Our wisdom and character, perhaps even our sanity, will be called into question. Our calling is not to do what is wise in the world's eyes, nor is it to take the popular course of action. Rather than wrangle with God, we are to submit to his leading, however "odd" it may seem.

DEVOTION

Lord, I want to become more sensitive to your leading, better able to discern your voice. I want to devote my days to doing your will, not pursuing my own agenda. No matter what it means, give me the courage to go everywhere you direct and do everything you instruct.

For more Bible passages on planning, see Psalm 33:10–11; Proverbs 15:22; 16:3, 9; 19:21; Isaiah 29:15; and James 4:13–14.

To complete the book of 2 Corinthians during this twelve-part study, read 2 Corinthians 1:12–2:13.

JOURNALING

What are your specific fears of turning over your personal calendar to God and saying, "Not my will, but your will be done"?

LESSON THREE

GOD'S NEW AGREEMENT

MAX
LUCADO

REFLECTION

Household standards. Civic ordinances. Congressional legislation. Life is full of rules and regulations. What were some of the hard and fast requirements you were forced to live by at home growing up or when you were in school? What were the consequences if you violated them?

SITUATION

After Paul left Corinth (Acts 18:18) to take the gospel to other cities, the young congregation began to listen to the teachings of some who questioned the message of Christ. These false teachers urged a return to the Jewish idea of trying to earn God's approval by keeping the law of Moses.

OBSERVATION

Read 2 Corinthians 3:4–18 from the NCV or the NKJV.

NCV

⁴We can say this, because through Christ we feel certain before God. ⁵We are not saying that we can do this work ourselves. It is God who makes us able to do all that we do. ⁶He made us able to be servants of a new agreement from himself to his people. This new agreement is not a written law, but it is of the Spirit. The written law brings death, but the Spirit gives life.

⁷*The law that brought death was written in words on stone. It came with God's glory, which made Moses' face so bright that the Israelites could not continue to look at it. But that glory later disappeared.* ⁸*So surely the new way that brings the Spirit has even more glory.* ⁹*If the law that judged people guilty of sin had glory, surely the new way that makes people right with God has much greater glory.* ¹⁰*That old law had glory, but it really loses its glory when it is compared to the much greater glory of this new way.* ¹¹*If that law which disappeared came with glory, then this new way which continues forever has much greater glory.*

¹²*We have this hope, so we are very bold.* ¹³*We are not like Moses, who put a covering over his face so the Israelites would not see it. The glory was disappearing, and Moses did not want them to see it end.* ¹⁴*But their minds were closed, and even today that same covering hides the meaning when they read the old agreement. That covering is taken away only through Christ.* ¹⁵*Even today, when they read the law of Moses, there is a covering over their minds.* ¹⁶*But when a person changes and follows the Lord, that covering is taken away.* ¹⁷*The Lord is the Spirit, and where the Spirit of the Lord is, there is freedom.* ¹⁸*Our faces, then, are not covered. We all show the Lord's glory, and we are being changed to be like him. This change in us brings ever greater glory, which comes from the Lord, who is the Spirit.*

NKJV

⁴*And we have such trust through Christ toward God.* ⁵*Not that we are sufficient of ourselves to think of anything as being from ourselves, but our sufficiency is from God,* ⁶*who also made us sufficient as ministers of the new covenant, not of the letter but of the Spirit; for the letter kills, but the Spirit gives life.*

⁷*But if the ministry of death, written and engraved on stones, was glorious, so that the children of Israel could not look steadily at the face of Moses because of the glory of his countenance, which glory was passing away,* ⁸*how will the ministry of the Spirit not be more glorious?* ⁹*For if the ministry of condemnation had glory, the ministry of righteousness exceeds much more in glory.* ¹⁰*For even what was made glorious had no glory in this respect, because of the glory that excels.* ¹¹*For if what is passing away was glorious, what remains is much more glorious.*

¹²*Therefore, since we have such hope, we use great boldness of speech—* ¹³*unlike Moses, who put a veil over his face so that the children of Israel could not look steadily at the end of what was passing away.* ¹⁴*But their minds were blinded. For until this day the same veil remains unlifted in the reading of the Old Testament, because the veil is taken away in Christ.* ¹⁵*But even to this day, when Moses is read, a veil lies on their heart.* ¹⁶*Nevertheless when one turns to the Lord, the veil is taken away.* ¹⁷*Now the Lord is the Spirit; and where the Spirit of the Lord is, there is liberty.* ¹⁸*But we all, with unveiled face, beholding as in a mirror the glory of the Lord, are being transformed into the same image from glory to glory, just as by the Spirit of the Lord.*

EXPLORATION

1. How would you explain the difference between the old covenant (divine rules written on tablets of stone) and the new covenant?

Heb 8: 1-13

2. Where does Paul say we can find the power to live as God expects?

Ep. 5-8-12

3. What revealing things does Paul say about the effect of God's law?

The old way (the Law) only condemns
it doesn't lead to sal.
new way Spirit gives life.

EX 34-28-35

4. Paul compares the inferior glory of the old covenant with the surpassing glory of God's new agreement. What exactly *is* glory?

revelation of God's truth - bothe in law & grace.

Ex 31-> 31-34

Law

5. Describe the difference between external pressure to do something and the internal desire to accomplish it.

- Law is external
- Holy Spirit - veil is taken away enables us to accomplish this

INSPIRATION

Where man fails God excels. Salvation comes from heaven downward, not earth upward. *"A new day from heaven will dawn upon us"* (Luke 1:78 NCV). *"Every good action and every perfect gift is from God"* (James 1:17).

Please note: Salvation is God-given, God-driven, God-empowered, and God-originated. The gift is not from man to God. It is from God to man. *"It is not our love for God; it is God's love for us in sending his Son to be the way to take away our sins"* (1 John 4:10).

Grace is created by God and given to man. *"Sky above, make victory fall like rain; clouds, pour down victory. Let the earth receive it, and let salvation grow, and let victory grow with it. I, the LORD, have created it"* (Isa. 45:8).

On the basis of this point alone, Christianity is set apart from any other religion in the world. "No other system, ideology or religion proclaims a free forgiveness and a new life to those who have done nothing to deserve it but deserve judgment instead" (John Stott, *Romans: God's Good News for the World*, 118).

To quote John MacArthur: "As far as the way of salvation is concerned, there are only two religions the world has ever known or will ever know—the religion of divine accomplishment, which is biblical Christianity, and the religion of human achievement, which includes all other kinds of religion, by whatever names they may go under" (John MacArthur, *The New Testament Commentary of Romans* [Chicago: Moody 1991], 199).

Every other approach to God is a bartering system; if I do this, God will do that. I'm either saved by works (what I do), emotions (what I experience), or knowledge (what I know).

By contrast, Christianity has no whiff of negotiation at all. Man is not the negotiator; indeed, man has no grounds from which to negotiate. (From *In the Grip of Grace* by Max Lucado)

REACTION

6. In what ways is the Christian explanation of salvation insulting or offensive to human pride? *to Be saved - must be totally depend on God.*

7. Someone has suggested that God's new covenant turns religious "have-to's" into spiritual "want-to's". How do you interpret this comment?

8. What part does the Holy Spirit play in God's new covenant? *He ilumates our understanding.*

9. What are some specific ways you have seen God's glorious Spirit work in your life since you put your faith in Christ?

- able to forgive more.
- boldness
- trust when you cannot see. in the silence
- to love + accept those you might not in yourself be drawn to.
- to listen more - give the "word" and not my own ideas.
- to

10. Paul mentions a kind of boldness we should have in being radiant before others. What does this mean? Because the vail of the is taken away - the Holy Spirit now can reveal truth to you.

11. Of the various blessings of the new covenant which Paul lists here—confidence, competence, righteousness, boldness, radiance, freedom—which do you sense the greatest need for in your life just now?

Discernment! between what I may want + when is Gods way/plan for me.

LIFE LESSONS

It's been said that the Christian life isn't merely difficult—it's *impossible*! Impossible, that is, without supernatural help. Imagine being asked to write a Shakespearean play, a three-act drama as brilliant as anything the writer ever penned. A ridiculous and unattainable assignment, right? Unless . . . unless, somehow the very spirit of Shakespeare could indwell you and write through you. Then the task *would* be possible. This is precisely what the new covenant promises: the Spirit of God coming to live within us. He makes us spiritually alive, gives us a new nature and new desires (2 Cor. 5:17). And with all that, he supplies new power to live as God commands.

DEVOTION

God, I praise you for the wonderful promise of the new covenant! What we were unable to do, you did. Show me more and more what grace really means. Grant me insight and humility so that I might really shine for you, reflecting your glory to others, and bringing you more glory in the process.

For more Bible passages on the new covenant, see Exodus 34:28–35; Jeremiah 31:33; Ezekiel 36:26; and Hebrews 8.

To complete the book of 2 Corinthians during this twelve-part study, read 2 Corinthians 2:14–3:18.

JOURNALING

What does real, God-honoring freedom look like in a believer's life?

LESSON FOUR

SOLI DEO GLORIA!

MAX LUCADO

REFLECTION

Motives. We all have them. We all have reasons (conscious and subconscious) for why we do what we do. What would you say are your dominant motivations in life . . . those compelling urges that prompt you during the average day?

SITUATION

An unnamed group of smooth-talking, slick-operating troublemakers had infiltrated the church at Corinth, bashing Paul and encouraging a departure from his new covenant gospel of grace. To prevent this terrible possibility, Paul contrasted his ministry and motives with theirs.

OBSERVATION

Read 2 Corinthians 4:1—18 from the NCV or the NKJV.

NCV

¹God, with his mercy, gave us this work to do, so we don't give up. ²But we have turned away from secret and shameful ways. We use no trickery, and we do not change the teaching of God. We teach the truth plainly, showing everyone who we are. Then they can know in their hearts what kind of people we are in God's sight. ³If the Good News that we preach is hidden, it is hidden only to those who are lost. ⁴The devil who rules this world has blinded the minds of those who do not believe. They cannot see the light of the Good News—the Good News about the glory of Christ, who is exactly like God. ⁵We do not preach about ourselves, but we preach that Jesus Christ is Lord and that we are your servants for Jesus. ⁶God once said, "Let the light shine out of the darkness!" This is the same God who made his light shine in our hearts by letting us know the glory of God that is in the face of Christ.

⁷We have this treasure from God, but we are like clay jars that hold the treasure. This shows that the great power is from God, not from us. ⁸We have troubles all around us, but we are not defeated. We do not know what to do, but we do not give up the hope of living. ⁹We are persecuted, but God does not leave us. We are hurt sometimes, but we are not destroyed. ¹⁰We carry the death of Jesus in our own bodies so that the life of Jesus can also be seen in our bodies. ¹¹We are alive, but for Jesus we are always in danger of death so that the life of Jesus can be seen in our bodies that die. ¹²So death is working in us, but life is working in you.

[13]It is written in the Scriptures, "I believed, so I spoke." Our faith is like this, too. We believe, and so we speak. [14]God raised the Lord Jesus from the dead, and we know that God will also raise us with Jesus. God will bring us together with you, and we will stand before him. [15]All these things are for you. And so the grace of God that is being given to more and more people will bring increasing thanks to God for his glory.

[16]So we do not give up. Our physical body is becoming older and weaker, but our spirit inside us is made new every day. [17]We have small troubles for a while now, but they are helping us gain an eternal glory that is much greater than the troubles. [18]We set our eyes not on what we see but on what we cannot see. What we see will last only a short time, but what we cannot see will last forever.

NKJV

[1]Therefore, since we have this ministry, as we have received mercy, we do not lose heart. [2]But we have renounced the hidden things of shame, not walking in craftiness nor handling the word of God deceitfully, but by manifestation of the truth commending ourselves to every man's conscience in the sight of God. [3]But even if our gospel is veiled, it is veiled to those who are perishing, [4]whose minds the god of this age has blinded, who do not believe, lest the light of the gospel of the glory of Christ, who is the image of God, should shine on them. [5]For we do not preach ourselves, but Christ Jesus the Lord, and ourselves your bondservants for Jesus' sake. [6]For it is the God who commanded light to shine out of darkness, who has shone in our hearts to give the light of the knowledge of the glory of God in the face of Jesus Christ.

[7]But we have this treasure in earthen vessels, that the excellence of the power may be of God and not of us. [8]We are hard-pressed on every side, yet not crushed; we are perplexed, but not in despair; [9]persecuted, but not forsaken; struck down, but not destroyed— [10]always carrying about in the body the dying of the Lord Jesus, that the life of Jesus also may be manifested in our body. [11]For we who live are always delivered to death for Jesus' sake, that the life of Jesus also may be manifested in our mortal flesh. [12]So then death is working in us, but life in you.

[13]And since we have the same spirit of faith, according to what is written, "I believed and therefore I spoke," we also believe and therefore speak, [14]knowing that He who raised up the Lord Jesus will also raise us up with Jesus, and will present us with you. [15]For all things are for your sakes, that grace, having spread through the many, may cause thanksgiving to abound to the glory of God.

[16]Therefore we do not lose heart. Even though our outward man is perishing, yet the inward man is being renewed day by day. [17]For our light affliction, which is but for a moment, is working for us a far more exceeding and eternal weight of glory, [18]while we do not look at the things which are seen, but at the things which are not seen. For the things which are seen are temporary, but the things which are not seen are eternal.

EXPLORATION

1. In a world that is obsessed with "image," it is always tempting to pretend, always tough to be authentic. Why is absolute honesty essential for those who serve God? *To be real to them*

2. What are some of the ways the devil blinds people to God's truth?

To look to people - faults
Yet just go

3. Why does Paul compare himself (and all Christians, actually) to "clay jars" (4:7 NCV) or "earthen vessels" (NKJV)?

4. Paul obviously lived a life full of trouble and hardship (see 1 Corinthians 4:9–13 and 2 Corinthians 6:4–10; 11:23–29). Why would God allow such difficulty for one of his most faithful servants? *Servant not above master to learn obedience.*

5. What silver lining does Paul see in his troubles?
To be more like Jesus

INSPIRATION

Moses asked to see it on Sinai.

It billowed through the temple, leaving priests too stunned to minister.

When Ezekiel saw it, he had to bow.

It encircled the angels and starstruck the shepherds in the Bethlehem pasture.

Jesus radiates it.

John beheld it.

Peter witnessed it on Transfiguration Hill.

Christ will return enthroned in it.

Heaven will be illuminated by it.

It gulfstreams the Atlantic of Scripture, touching every person with the potential of changing every life. Including yours. One glimpse, one taste, one sampling, and your faith will never be the same . . .

Glory.

God's glory.

To seek God's glory is to pray, "Thicken the air with your presence; make it misty with your majesty. Part heaven's drape and let your nature spill forth. God, show us God . . .

The Hebrew term for *glory* descends from a root word meaning heavy, weighty, or important. God's glory, then, celebrates his significance, his uniqueness, his one-of-a-kindness. As Moses prayed, "Who among the gods is like you, O LORD? Who is like you—majestic in holiness, awesome in glory, working wonders?" (Exod. 15:11 NIV).

When you think "God's glory," think "preeminence." And when you think "preeminence," think "priority." For God's glory is God's priority.

God's staff meetings, if he had them, would revolve around one question: "How can we reveal my glory today?" God's to-do list consists of one item: "Reveal my glory." Heaven's framed and mounted purpose statement hangs in the angels' break room just above the angel food cake. It reads: "Declare God's glory."

God exists to showcase God. (From *It's Not About Me* by Max Lucado)

REACTION

6. People were created to live for God's glory (Isa. 43:7), but in reality this is not most people's primary concern. What *are* they living for? themselves

7. What is the treasure we have from God (v. 7) and what are we supposed to do with it? show His glory

8. In this chapter Paul makes a big deal about speaking for and about God. How much do you do this in your life?

9. Other passages also speak of Christians "shining" for God (i.e., Matt. 5:14–16; Phil. 2:15). What does this look like in everyday, practical terms?

Godly life refects Christ

10. *Soli Deo gloria* means "to the glory of God alone." What are some indications that a believer has embraced such a mind-set and lifestyle?

Not easily offended
Does not seek his own glory
willing to put self in background

11. What are three specific acts you can commit to that will shine the glory of Christ into your world? *Willing to Listen to others with sincerety Loving the unlovely*

LIFE LESSONS

You can get attention by being slick and flashy and by cultivating a certain "image," but you'll never have a deep impact on others that way. The most powerful and eternally significant lives are those, like Paul, who realize they are mere vessels who have been filled with a heaven-sent treasure. They realize God is the point, not them. According to the Bible, we exist to bring God glory, to shine for him, to point others to him. Like John the Baptist we need to say, "He must become greater, and I must become less important" (John 3:30 NCV). Focus today on the substance of your life more so than on mere style. Spiritual depth, authenticity, faithfulness—these are the qualities that honor God and cause others to stop and stare.

DEVOTION

Father, forgive me for my tendency to think more highly of myself than I should. Forgive me for the times I pursue my agenda and fail to put you first. Remind me that I'm a clay pot containing the treasure of the gospel. Give me an eternal perspective, so that I am more motivated to live for your glory.

For more Bible passages on living for God's glory, see Exodus 33:12–23; 1 Chronicles 16:24; 2 Chronicles 7:1–3; Psalm 57; Psalm 115:1; and 1 Corinthians 10:31.

To complete the book of 2 Corinthians during this twelve-part study, read 2 Corinthians 4:1–15.

JOURNALING

How can you embrace more God-honoring motives and abandon less worthy
ones?

LESSON FIVE

ETERNAL
PERSPECTIVE

MAX
LUCADO

REFLECTION

More people than ever are living long enough to celebrate their one hundredth birthdays. But even a century in this world is still just a blip when we compare it to an eternity in the next. When in your life have you had the most acute sense of "this life is not all there is"?

SITUATION

To counter the allegations of some false teachers in Corinth, Paul shares openly his deepest beliefs and his true motives for serving Christ. As he defends his ministry and message, we get a window in the heart and mind of this great apostle who lived each day with eternity in view.

OBSERVATION

Read 2 Corinthians 4:16– 5:10 from the NCV or the NKJV.

NCV

16So we do not give up. Our physical body is becoming older and weaker, but our spirit inside us is made new every day. 17We have small troubles for a while now, but they are helping us gain an eternal glory that is much greater than the troubles. 18We set our eyes not on what we see but on what we cannot see. What we see will last only a short time, but what we cannot see will last forever.

5:1We know that our body—the tent we live in here on earth—will be destroyed. But when that happens, God will have a house for us. It will not be a house made by human hands; instead, it will be a home in heaven that will last forever. 2But now we groan in this tent. We want God to give us our heavenly home, 3because it will clothe us so we will not be naked. 4While we live in this body, we have burdens, and we groan. We do not want to be naked, but we want to be clothed with our heavenly home. Then this body that dies will be fully covered with life. 5This is what God made us for, and he has given us the Spirit to be a guarantee for this new life.

⁶So we always have courage. We know that while we live in this body, we are away from the Lord. ⁷We live by what we believe, not by what we can see. ⁸So I say that we have courage. We really want to be away from this body and be at home with the Lord. ⁹Our only goal is to please God whether we live here or there, ¹⁰because we must all stand before Christ to be judged. Each of us will receive what we should get—good or bad—for the things we did in the earthly body.

NKJV

¹⁶Therefore we do not lose heart. Even though our outward man is perishing, yet the inward man is being renewed day by day. ¹⁷For our light affliction, which is but for a moment, is working for us a far more exceeding and eternal weight of glory, ¹⁸while we do not look at the things which are seen, but at the things which are not seen. For the things which are seen are temporary, but the things which are not seen are eternal.

⁵:¹For we know that if our earthly house, this tent, is destroyed, we have a building from God, a house not made with hands, eternal in the heavens. ²For in this we groan, earnestly desiring to be clothed with our habitation which is from heaven, ³if indeed, having been clothed, we shall not be found naked. ⁴For we who are in this tent groan, being burdened, not because we want to be unclothed, but further clothed, that mortality may be swallowed up by life. ⁵Now He who has prepared us for this very thing is God, who also has given us the Spirit as a guarantee.

⁶So we are always confident, knowing that while we are at home in the body we are absent from the Lord. ⁷For we walk by faith, not by sight. ⁸We are confident, yes, well pleased rather to be absent from the body and to be present with the Lord.

⁹Therefore we make it our aim, whether present or absent, to be well pleasing to Him. ¹⁰For we must all appear before the judgment seat of Christ, that each one may receive the things done in the body, according to what he has done, whether good or bad.

EXPLORATION

1. What kept Paul going through the hard times of life and ministry?

Knowing the future with Christ the Holy spirit

2. What does it mean to "set our eyes" or to "look . . . at the things which are not seen"? How can you personally apply this to your life?

KNOWing that Enernity is forever

3. What does Paul mean by comparing our earthly bodies to tents?

only temporarly

4. How can we balance longing for heaven while still accomplishing God's purposes for us here on earth? *Paul as an example Holding loose to earthly things*

5. If God forgets our sins once we are forgiven under the terms of the new covenant (Jer. 31:34), why does Paul mention the judgment seat of Christ?

FoR Christians - Rewards for works done.
(Beama)

INSPIRATION

You've probably heard the story of the couple who resorted to do-it-yourself marriage counseling. They resolved to make a list of each other's faults and then read them aloud. Sounds like a constructive evening, don't you think? So she made hers and he made his. The wife gave her list of complaints to the husband and he read them aloud. "You snore, you eat in bed, you get home too late and up too early . . ." After finishing, the husband did the same. He gave her his list. But when she looked at the paper, she began to smile. He, too, had written his grievances, but next to each he had written, "I forgive this."

The result was a tabulated list of grace.

You'll receive such a list on judgment day. Remember the primary purpose of judgment: to reveal the grace of the Father. As your sins are announced, God's grace is magnified.

Imagine the event. You are before the judgment seat of Christ. The book is opened and the reading begins—each sin, each deceit, each occasion of destruction and greed. But as soon as the infraction is read, grace is proclaimed.

Disrespected parents at age thirteen.

Shaded the truth at age fifteen.

Gossiped at age twenty-six.

Lusted at age thirty.

Disregarded the leading of the Spirit at age forty.

Disobeyed God's word at age fifty-two.

The result? God's merciful verdict will echo through the universe. For the first time in history, we will understand the depth of his goodness. Itemized grace. Catalogued kindness. Registered forgiveness. We will stand in awe as one sin after another is proclaimed, and then pardoned. Jealousies revealed, then removed. Infidelities announced, then cleansed. Lies exposed, then erased . . .

What a triumph this will be for our Master!

Perhaps you're thinking, *It will be triumph for him, but humiliation for me.* No, it won't. Scripture promises, *"The one who trusts in him will never be put to shame"* (1 Pet. 2:6 NIV) . . .

Shame is a child of self-centeredness. Heaven's occupants are not self-centered, they are Christ-centered. You will be in your sinless state. The sinless don't protect a reputation or project an image. You won't be ashamed. You'll be happy to let God do in heaven what he did on earth—be honored in your weaknesses.

Heads bowed in shame? No. Heads bowed in worship? No doubt. (From *When Christ Comes* by Max Lucado)

REACTION

6. The judgment seat of Christ will also be a place of eternal reward for faithful believers. What kinds of reward should we expect? (Hint: see Matthew 25:21–23; 1 Corinthians 4:5; 1 Peter 1:4; 1 Corinthians 9:25–27; James 1:12; 2 Timothy 4:8)

7. How do you act knowing that someday you will stand before Christ and be held accountable for your actions? *Godly - selfless*

8. How is it possible for today's troubles to produce eternal glory?

By the Lords way - scripture

9. How will our eternal resurrected bodies differ from our current bodies?

No Longer Gini

10. Besides giving us power, what does the presence of the Spirit in our lives promise? ASSURANCE & peace

11. What are three specific changes you need to make so that you can honestly say, "My 'only goal is to please God'"?

LIFE LESSONS

A clear and compelling vision of the future does have real power to affect our actions in the present. Think of the student who stands to get a scholarship if he can achieve a certain SAT score next month, the bride-to-be who wants to fit into her wedding gown in six weeks, the hardworking couple who is absolutely committed to the goal of retiring by age fifty. The apostle Paul was riveted by the reality of eternity—the judgment seat of Christ helped him shape his behavior; the promise of heaven gave him real hope when life's circumstances turned unpleasant. By cultivating a mind-set that continually recalls these easy-to-forget realities (Col. 3:2), we become the people God made us to be, and our lives take on new power and purpose.

DEVOTION

Lord, I confess how quickly I lose sight of ultimate realities, and how easily I become immersed in temporal events. Thank you for Paul's valuable reminder that this life is not all there is. Thank you for the promise of heaven. Show me how to set my mind on things above, not on the things that are on the earth.

For more Bible passages on eternal perspective, see Job 19:25–27; Psalm 73:24–26; John 15:1–4; 1 Thessalonians 4:13–18; and Revelation 21–22.

To complete the book of 2 Corinthians during this twelve-part study, read 2 Corinthians 4:16–5:21.

JOURNALING

C. S. Lewis suggested that the people who do the most in this world are those who think the most of the next world. When have you been most motivated and energized by an eternal perspective?

LESSON SIX

LIVING AS A
SERVANT

MAX
LUCADO

REFLECTION

Perhaps you've heard the old saying "If you were arrested and put on trial for being a devoted follower of Christ, would there be enough evidence to convict you?" What are the biggest changes you've seen God bring forth in your life since you put your faith in Jesus? *persevere*

SITUATION

To protect the gospel, Paul defends himself (a messenger of the gospel) from the slanderous attacks of the false teachers who have infiltrated Corinth. As the apostle reminds his readers of his life and conduct in their midst (including much hardship), we get a glimpse of ultimate servanthood.

OBSERVATION

Read 2 Corinthians 6:1–10 from the NCV or the NKJV.

NCV

¹We are workers together with God, so we beg you: Do not let the grace that you received from God be for nothing. ²God says,

"At the right time I heard your prayers.

On the day of salvation I helped you."

I tell you that the "right time" is now, and the "day of salvation" is now.

³We do not want anyone to find fault with our work, so nothing we do will be a problem for anyone. ⁴But in every way we show we are servants of God: in accepting many hard things, in troubles, in difficulties, and in great problems. ⁵We are beaten and thrown into prison. We meet those who become upset with us and start riots. We work hard, and sometimes we get no sleep or food. ⁶We show we are servants of God by our pure lives, our understanding, patience, and kindness, by the Holy Spirit, by true love, ⁷by speaking the truth, and by God's power. We use our right living to defend ourselves against everything. ⁸Some people honor us, but others blame us. Some people say evil things about us, but others say good things. Some people say we are liars, but we speak the truth. ⁹We are not known, but we are well known. We seem to be dying, but we continue to live. We are punished, but we are not killed. ¹⁰We have much sadness, but we are always rejoicing. We are poor, but we are making many people rich in faith. We have nothing, but really we have everything.

NKJV

¹We then, as workers together with Him also plead with you not to receive the grace of God in vain. ²For He says:

"In an acceptable time I have heard you,

And in the day of salvation I have helped you."

Behold, now is the accepted time; behold, now is the day of salvation.

³We give no offense in anything, that our ministry may not be blamed. ⁴But in all things we commend ourselves as ministers of God: in much patience, in tribulations, in needs, in distresses, ⁵in stripes, in imprisonments, in tumults, in labors, in sleeplessness, in fastings; ⁶by purity, by knowledge, by longsuffering, by kindness, by the Holy Spirit, by sincere love, ⁷by the word of truth, by the power of God, by the armor of righteousness on the right hand and on the left, ⁸by honor and dishonor, by evil report and good report; as deceivers, and yet true; ⁹as unknown, and yet well known; as dying, and behold we live; as chastened, and yet not killed; ¹⁰as sorrowful, yet always rejoicing; as poor, yet making many rich; as having nothing, and yet possessing all things.

EXPLORATION

1. Paul describes himself (and his colleagues) as "workers together with God" (v. 1 NCV) and "servants of God" (v. 4 NCV). What's the difference?

work side by side - But under God

2. What does it mean to receive God's grace in vain?

not to hoard it.

3. Paul faced no shortage of trouble and suffering in service to the gospel. What conclusion does Paul draw from his trials? *Looked to eternity was no*

4. How can a believer endure such constant affliction and opposition and keep going? Word -

5. How does living a blameless life give you freedom?

INSPIRATION

Every day do something you don't want to do. Pick up someone else's trash. Surrender your parking place. Call the long-winded relative. Carry the cooler. Doesn't have to be a big thing. Helen Keller once told the Tennessee legislature that when she was young, she had longed to do great things and could not, so she decided to do small things in a great way. Don't be too big to do something small. *"Throw yourselves into the work of the Master, confident that nothing you do for him is a waste of time or effort"* (1 Cor. 15:58 MSG).

Baron de Rothschild once asked artist Ary Scheffer to paint his portrait. Though a wealthy financier, Rothschild posed as a beggar, wearing rags and holding a tin cup. During one day of painting, a friend of the artist entered the room. Thinking Rothschild was really a beggar, he dropped a coin in his cup.

Ten years later that man received a letter from Baron de Rothschild and a check for ten thousand francs. The message read, "You one day gave a coin to Baron de Rothschild in the studio of Ary Scheffer. He has invested it and today sends you the capital which you entrusted to him, together with the compounded interest. A good action always brings a good fortune."

We would add to that line. A good action not only brings a good fortune, it brings God's attention. He notices the actions of servants. He sent his Son to be one. (From *Cure for the Common Life* by Max Lucado)

REACTION

6. Why are so many Christians so reluctant to roll up their sleeves and minister to others? Selfish

7. As Paul describes his complicated, roller-coaster life as a committed servant of Christ, what ironies or paradoxes does he cite?

as known + yet unknown
dying,
sorrowful

8. Some readers protest, "Paul's words really only apply to full-time ministers. The average Christian can't be expected to live like this." How do you respond?

9. Paul was devoted to living in such a way that his life did not contradict the gospel. What attitudes, values, actions, or habits in your life might tarnish the reputation of Christ or his church?

10. Why does God allow his choicest servants to undergo so much affliction?

11. Why, in the final analysis, does being a servant matter so much?

to reflect christ

LIFE LESSONS

The more Adam and Eve pondered the lies of the evil one, the more they doubted the goodness of God. Finally, declaring their independence, they struck out on their own to try to find "life"—to make it work without God. They would do this by trying to control situations and people. And aren't we chips off the old block? Don't we tend to approach life the same way? Enter Jesus, who says, "Those who want to save their lives will give up true life, and those who give up their lives for me will have true life" (Matt. 16:25 NCV). In other words, the path to joy and fulfillment isn't found in control; it is found in surrender. Those who choose to be servants of God, giving up control and yielding fully to his will and his work, are those who find true life—now and forever.

DEVOTION

Father, I can either live selfishly, saying, "My will be done," or I can live as a servant, saying, "Thy will be done." Please change me. Make me more like Paul, more like your own Son, Christ. Remind me that I'm not my own, that I have been bought at a price.

For more Bible passages on servanthood, see Matthew 10:24–25; 20:26; Luke 19:17; John 15:20; and Philippians 2:5–11.

To complete the book of 2 Corinthians during this twelve-part study, read 2 Corinthians 6:1–7:1.

JOURNALING

How is 1 Peter 4:10–11 related to the passage in this chapter, and how can you
live it out in your daily life?

LESSON SEVEN

FOLLOW THE LEADER

MAX LUCADO

REFLECTION

Go into a bookstore and take note of all the titles that have to do with *leadership*. Clearly this is a hot topic! In your opinion what are the qualities that make for the best leaders?

SITUATION

Paul established the church at Corinth on his second missionary journey. A short time later, some self-appointed "apostles" infiltrated the flock and launched an effort to gain control of it by slandering Paul's character and attacking his message of grace. His response provides us some great lessons in leadership.

OBSERVATION

Read 2 Corinthians 7:2–16 from the NCV or the NKJV.

NCV

²Open your hearts to us. We have not done wrong to anyone, we have not ruined the faith of anyone, and we have not cheated anyone. ³I do not say this to blame you. I told you before that we love you so much we would live or die with you. ⁴I feel very sure of you and am very proud of you. You give me much comfort, and in all of our troubles I have great joy.

⁵When we came into Macedonia, we had no rest. We found trouble all around us. We had fighting on the outside and fear on the inside. ⁶But God, who comforts those who are troubled, comforted us when Titus came. ⁷We were comforted, not only by his coming but also by the comfort you gave him. Titus told us about your wish to see me and that you are very sorry for what you did. He also told me about your great care for me, and when I heard this, I was much happier.

8Even if my letter made you sad, I am not sorry I wrote it. At first I was sorry, because it made you sad, but you were sad only for a short time. 9Now I am happy, not because you were made sad, but because your sorrow made you change your lives. You became sad in the way God wanted you to, so you were not hurt by us in any way. 10The kind of sorrow God wants makes people change their hearts and lives. This leads to salvation, and you cannot be sorry for that. But the kind of sorrow the world has brings death. 11See what this sorrow—the sorrow God wanted you to have—has done to you: It has made you very serious. It made you want to prove you were not wrong. It made you angry and afraid. It made you want to see me. It made you care. It made you want the right thing to be done. You proved you were innocent in the problem. 12I wrote that letter, not because of the one who did the wrong or because of the person who was hurt. I wrote the letter so you could see, before God, the great care you have for us. 13That is why we were comforted.

Not only were we very comforted, we were even happier to see that Titus was so happy. All of you made him feel much better. 14I bragged to Titus about you, and you showed that I was right. Everything we said to you was true, and you have proved that what we bragged about to Titus is true. 15And his love for you is stronger when he remembers that you were all ready to obey. You welcomed him with respect and fear. 16I am very happy that I can trust you fully.

NKJV

2Open your hearts to us. We have wronged no one, we have corrupted no one, we have cheated no one. 3I do not say this to condemn; for I have said before that you are in our hearts, to die together and to live together. 4Great is my boldness of speech toward you, great is my boasting on your behalf. I am filled with comfort. I am exceedingly joyful in all our tribulation.

5For indeed, when we came to Macedonia, our bodies had no rest, but we were troubled on every side. Outside were conflicts, inside were fears. 6Nevertheless God, who comforts the downcast, comforted us by the coming of Titus, 7and not only by his coming, but also by the consolation with which he was comforted in you, when he told us of your earnest desire, your mourning, your zeal for me, so that I rejoiced even more.

8For even if I made you sorry with my letter, I do not regret it; though I did regret it. For I perceive that the same epistle made you sorry, though only for a while. 9Now I rejoice, not that you were made sorry, but that your sorrow led to repentance. For you were made sorry in a godly manner, that you might suffer loss from us in nothing. 10For godly sorrow produces repentance leading to salvation, not to be regretted; but the sorrow of the world produces death. 11For observe this very thing, that you sorrowed in a godly manner: What diligence it produced in you, what clearing of yourselves, what indignation, what fear, what vehement desire, what zeal, what vindication! In all things you proved yourselves to be clear in this matter. 12Therefore, although I wrote to you, I did not do it for the sake of him who had done the wrong, nor for the sake of him who suffered wrong, but that our care for you in the sight of God might appear to you.

¹³Therefore we have been comforted in your comfort. And we rejoiced exceedingly more for the joy of Titus, because his spirit has been refreshed by you all. ¹⁴For if in anything I have boasted to him about you, I am not ashamed. But as we spoke all things to you in truth, even so our boasting to Titus was found true. ¹⁵And his affections are greater for you as he remembers the obedience of you all, how with fear and trembling you received him. ¹⁶Therefore I rejoice that I have confidence in you in everything.

EXPLORATION

1. How does Paul's defense here correspond to Jesus' classic statement, "You will know these people by what they do" (Matt. 7:16 NCV)?

2. What are some ways a leader can lose the trust of his or her followers?

3. What valuable lessons about confrontation do you find here?

4. Paul mentions being proud of the Corinthians (v. 4). When is the last time a leader or authority figure made such comments to you? How did those words affect you?

5. What is godly sorrow?

INSPIRATION

Peer into the prison and see him for yourself: bent and frail, shackled to the arm of a Roman guard. Behold the apostle of God. Who knows when his back last felt a bed or his mouth knew a good meal? Three decades of travel and trouble, and what's he got to show for it?

There's squabbling in Philippi, competition in Corinth, the legalists are swarming in Galatia. Crete is plagued by money-grabbers. Ephesus is stalked by womanizers. Even some of Paul's own friends have turned against him.

Dead broke. No family. No property. Nearsighted and worn out.

Oh, he had his moments. Spoke to an emperor once, but couldn't convert him. Gave a lecture at an Areopagus men's club, but wasn't asked to speak there again. Spent a few days with Peter and the boys in Jerusalem, but they couldn't seem to get along, so Paul hit the road.

And never got off. Ephesus, Thessalonica, Athens, Syracuse, Malta. The only list longer than his itinerary was his misfortune. Got stoned in one city and stranded in another. Nearly drowned as many times as he nearly starved. If he spent more than one week in the same place, it was probably a prison.

He never received a salary. Had to pay his own travel expenses. Kept a part-time job on the side to make ends meet.

Doesn't look like a hero.

Doesn't sound like one either. He introduced himself as the worst sinner in history. He was a Christian-killer before he was a Christian leader. At times his heart was so heavy, Paul's pen drug itself across the page. *What a miserable man I am! Who will save me from this body that brings me death?* (Rom. 7:24 NCV).

Only heaven knows how long he stared at the question before he found the courage to defy logic and write, *I thank God for saving me through Jesus Christ our Lord!* (Rom. 7:25).

One minute he's in charge; the next he's in doubt. One day he's preaching; the next he's in prison. And that's where I'd like you to look at him. Look at him in the prison.

Pretend you don't know him. You're a guard or a cook or a friend of the hatchet man, and you've come to get one last look at the guy while they sharpen the blade.

What you see shuffling around in his cell isn't too much. But what I lean over and tell you is: "That man will shape the course of history." (From *When God Whispers Your Name* by Max Lucado)

REACTION

size, appearance

6. What are the things that made Paul an unlikely leader? What qualities or experiences equipped him for such amazing service as an apostle?

spirit, vision educated

7. If you could ask Paul any question, what would it be?

how he endured his physical suffering!

8. The Corinthians were Paul's "problem" church. He confronted them repeatedly. What gives someone the authority and the confidence to confront another?

9. Someone has said that repentance isn't just being sorry . . . it's being sorry enough to change. Comment on that thought.

10. When is the last time a leader confronted you? What happened?

11. How specifically can you be a better follower to those who lead you?

LIFE LESSONS

If a leader is one who influences others to go in a specific direction and to achieve certain goals, then everyone can and should be a leader. A dad should impact his family. A third grader can lead his classmates in a healthy direction. A stay-at-home mom can make a difference in the lives of her neighbors. A middle manager can affect those in his or her office. Paul's example reminds us that effective, God-honoring leadership is rooted in honesty, integrity, genuine concern, courage, and straightforward communication. Everyone has the capacity to lead someone else, and everyone has the need also to follow another. Remember, the one who is unwilling to follow is unfit to lead.

DEVOTION

Father, thank you for the strong leaders you've put in my life. None of them are perfect, but all have strengths from which I can benefit. Remind me often to pray for them and give me opportunities to encourage them in tangible, concrete ways.

For more Bible passages on biblical leadership, see Titus 1; 1 Timothy 3:1–13; and Hebrews 13:17.

To complete the book of 2 Corinthians during this twelve-part study, read 2 Corinthians 7:2–16.

JOURNALING

The previous lesson focused on being a *servant*; this current lesson looks at some principles of *leadership*. How are those two things related?

LESSON EIGHT

MONEY
MATTERS

MAX
LUCADO

REFLECTION

Passing the plate . . . asking for money . . . sermons on tithing . . . Can you think of a single topic that generates more raised eyebrows, more tension, or more shakes of the head than this one? Why is giving such a sore subject for so many Christians?

SITUATION

Having defended his character and his ministry from vicious attacks, Paul asked the Corinthian believers to complete a collection promised a year earlier for the poverty-stricken church in Jerusalem. These chapters comprise the lengthiest and most detailed teaching on giving in the New Testament.

OBSERVATION

Read 2 Corinthians 9:1–15 from the NCV or the NKJV.

NCV

¹I really do not need to write you about this help for God's people. ²I know you want to help. I have been bragging about this to the people in Macedonia, telling them that you in Southern Greece have been ready to give since last year. And your desire to give has made most of them ready to give also. ³But I am sending the brothers to you so that our bragging about you in this will not be empty words. I want you to be ready, as I said you would be. ⁴If any of the people from Macedonia come with me and find that you are not ready, we will be ashamed that we were so sure of you. (And you will be ashamed, too!) ⁵So I thought I should ask these brothers to go to you before we do. They will finish getting in order the generous gift you promised so it will be ready when we come. And it will be a generous gift—not one that you did not want to give.

⁶Remember this: The person who plants a little will have a small harvest, but the person who plants a lot will have a big harvest. ⁷Each one should give as you have decided in your heart to give. You should not be sad when you give, and you should not give because you feel forced to give. God loves the person who gives happily. ⁸And God can give you more blessings than you need. Then you will always have plenty of every-thing—enough to give to every good work. ⁹It is written in the Scriptures:

"He gives freely to the poor.

The things he does are right and will continue forever."

[10]*God is the One who gives seed to the farmer and bread for food. He will give you all the seed you need and make it grow so there will be a great harvest from your goodness.* [11]*He will make you rich in every way so that you can always give freely. And your giving through us will cause many to give thanks to God.* [12]*This service you do not only helps the needs of God's people, it also brings many more thanks to God.* [13]*It is a proof of your faith. Many people will praise God because you obey the Good News of Christ—the gospel you say you believe—and because you freely share with them and with all others.* [14]*And when they pray, they will wish they could be with you because of the great grace that God has given you.* [15]*Thanks be to God for his gift that is too wonderful for words.*

NKJV

[1]*Now concerning the ministering to the saints, it is superfluous for me to write to you;* [2]*for I know your willingness, about which I boast of you to the Macedonians, that Achaia was ready a year ago; and your zeal has stirred up the majority.* [3]*Yet I have sent the brethren, lest our boasting of you should be in vain in this respect, that, as I said, you may be ready;* [4]*lest if some Macedonians come with me and find you unprepared, we (not to mention you!) should be ashamed of this confident boasting.* [5]*Therefore I thought it necessary to exhort the brethren to go to you ahead of time, and prepare your generous gift beforehand, which you had previously promised, that it may be ready as a matter of generosity and not as a grudging obligation.*

[6]*But this I say: He who sows sparingly will also reap sparingly, and he who sows bountifully will also reap bountifully.* [7]*So let each one give as he purposes in his heart, not grudgingly or of necessity; for God loves a cheerful giver.* [8]*And God is able to make all grace abound toward you, that you, always having all sufficiency in all things, may have an abundance for every good work.* [9]*As it is written:*

"He has dispersed abroad,

He has given to the poor;

His righteousness endures forever."

[10]*Now may He who supplies seed to the sower, and bread for food, supply and multiply the seed you have sown and increase the fruits of your righteousness,* [11]*while you are enriched in everything for all liberality, which causes thanksgiving through us to God.* [12]*For the administration of this service not only supplies the needs of the saints, but also is abounding through many thanksgivings to God,* [13]*while, through the proof of this ministry, they glorify God for the obedience of your confession to the gospel of Christ, and for your liberal sharing with them and all men,* [14]*and by their prayer for you, who long for you because of the exceeding grace of God in you.* [15]*Thanks be to God for His indescribable gift!*

EXPLORATION

1. Let's get right down to numbers. What amount or percentage of their income does Paul say Christians should give? *generously*

2. We all have thoughts like, "Boy, I could definitely use this money to pay a couple of bills!" Why should we give anyway?

3. In what ways does giving demonstrate faith?

4. What about the teaching that if you give away a lot, God will give you back a lot? How, if at all, does this passage support the idea that you "can't outgive God"?

5. A lot of people—but not the Macedonian Christians mentioned in these chapters—are quick to say they don't give much (or at all), because they don't have much. Is this a legitimate excuse?

INSPIRATION

Are you hoping that a change in circumstances will bring a change in your attitude? If so, you are in prison, and you need to learn a secret of traveling light. *What you have in your Shepherd is greater than what you don't have in life.*

May I meddle for a moment? What is the one thing separating you from joy? How do you fill in this blank: "I will be happy when _____"? When I am healed. When I am promoted. When I am married. When I am single. When I am rich. How would you finish that statement?

Now, with your answer firmly in mind, answer this. If your ship never comes in, if your dream never comes true, if the situation never changes, could you be happy? If not, then you are sleeping in the cold cell of discontent. You are in prison. And you need to know what you have in your Shepherd.

You have a God who hears you, the power of love behind you, the Holy Spirit within you, and all of heaven ahead of you. If you have the Shepherd, you have grace for every sin, direction for every turn, a candle for every corner, and an anchor for every storm. You have everything you need. (From *Traveling Light* by Max Lucado)

REACTION

6. How specifically does a Christian move from greediness to generosity?

7. What five words would you use to describe your current giving habits?

8. How do you determine what churches, ministries, or missionaries to support and how much to give?

9. Is it possible to give too much or to an unwise degree? How so?

10. Why do some people get unexpected money and automatically think of giving, while others get unanticipated windfalls and immediately think of spending?

11. What advice would you give to a Christian who acknowledged, "I know I need to be giving to the Lord's work, but how do I start when I've got so many bills already"?

LIFE LESSONS

When it comes to money, most folks tend to think, "Woohoo! What can I buy?!" Then, if there's anything left over (which is rare), they perhaps save or give a little bit. There's a better way, a more biblical financial model: give first, save second, and spend third. Imagine the really long-term implications of such a plan. Imagine arriving in heaven and discovering hundreds there because you used earthly wealth to help people grasp eternal truth. But not only that, realize how much less stressful your life would be here and now if you embarked on a disciplined savings plan—saving for upcoming expenses and emergencies, and for retirement. By curtailing your spending (something we all could stand to do), you eliminate the likelihood of piling up consumer debt. It's not rocket science. Mishandling money robs us of joy. Managing it well, so that we can be more generous, leads to rich blessing.

DEVOTION

God, as I think about money and how to handle it in a way that honors you, give me faith to believe the words of Jesus—that it is more blessed to give than to receive. I want to become more generous, quicker to open up my wallet or checkbook. Help me. Change me.

For more Bible passages on giving, see Deuteronomy 15:10–11; Malachi 3:8; Matthew 10:8; Luke 6:38; Romans 12:8; Acts 20:35; and 1 Timothy 6:17–19.

To complete the book of 2 Corinthians during this twelve-part study, read 2 Corinthians 8:1–9:15.

JOURNALING

Lately, when presented with opportunities to give, I . . .

LESSON NINE

GROUND
ZERO

MAX
LUCADO

REFLECTION

Pick any topic, situation, or dilemma—for example, divorce, parenting, money management, how to handle conflict, etc. Consider how many different (and often opposing) viewpoints people have on all such issues of life. Why the wide discrepancy? Most importantly, how can a person know the right or wisest perspective and the best course of action?

SITUATION

Because some rival preachers had entered Corinth and tried to discredit Paul and his gospel of grace, Paul felt compelled to defend his ministry and message. In the process, he reminds us that beneath the disputes of our lives, a deeper cosmic battle is underway—a battle for our minds.

OBSERVATION

Read 2 Corinthians 10:1–18 from the NCV or the NKJV.

NCV

[1]I, Paul, am begging you with the gentleness and the kindness of Christ. Some people say that I am easy on you when I am with you and bold when I am away. [2]They think we live in a worldly way, and I plan to be very bold with them when I come. I beg you that when I come I will not need to use that same boldness with you. [3]We do live in the world, but we do not fight in the same way the world fights. [4]We fight with weapons that are different from those the world uses. Our weapons have power from God that can destroy the enemy's strong places. We destroy people's arguments [5]and every proud thing that raises itself against the knowledge of God. We capture every thought and make it give up and obey Christ. [6]We are ready to punish anyone there who does not obey, but first we want you to obey fully.

[7]You must look at the facts before you. If you feel sure that you belong to Christ, you must remember that we belong to Christ just as you do. [8]It is true that we brag freely about the authority the Lord gave us. But this authority is to build you up, not to tear you down. So I will not be ashamed. [9]I do not want you to think I am trying to scare you with my letters. [10]Some people say, "Paul's letters are powerful and sound important, but when he is with us, he is weak. And his speaking is nothing." [11]They should know this: We are not there with you now, so we say these things in letters. But when we are there with you, we will show the same authority that we show in our letters.

[12]We do not dare to compare ourselves with those who think they are very important. They use themselves to measure themselves, and they judge themselves by what they themselves are. This shows that they know nothing. [13]But we will not brag about things outside the work that was given us to do. We will limit our bragging to the work that God gave us, and this includes our work with you. [14]We are not bragging too much, as we would be if we had not already come to you. But we have come to you with the Good News of Christ. [15]We limit our bragging to the work that is ours, not what others have done. We hope that as your faith continues to grow, you will help our work to grow much larger. [16]We want to tell the Good News in the areas beyond your city. We do not want to brag about work that has already been done in another person's area. [17]But, "If someone wants to brag, he should brag only about the Lord." [18]It is not those who say they are good who are accepted but those who the Lord thinks are good.

NKJV

[1]Now I, Paul, myself am pleading with you by the meekness and gentleness of Christ— who in presence am lowly among you, but being absent am bold toward you. [2]But I beg you that when I am present I may not be bold with that confidence by which I intend to be bold against some, who think of us as if we walked according to the flesh. [3]For though we walk in the flesh, we do not war according to the flesh. [4]For the weapons of our warfare are not carnal but mighty in God for pulling down strongholds, [5]casting down arguments and every high thing that exalts itself against the knowledge of God, bringing every thought into captivity to the obedience of Christ, [6]and being ready to punish all disobedience when your obedience is fulfilled.

[7]Do you look at things according to the outward appearance? If anyone is convinced in himself that he is Christ's, let him again consider this in himself, that just as he is Christ's, even so we are Christ's. [8]For even if I should boast somewhat more about our authority, which the Lord gave us for edification and not for your destruction, I shall not be ashamed— [9]lest I seem to terrify you by letters. [10]"For his letters," they say, "are weighty and powerful, but his bodily presence is weak, and his speech contemptible." [11]Let such a person consider this, that what we are in word by letters when we are absent, such we will also be in deed when we are present.

[12]For we dare not class ourselves or compare ourselves with those who commend themselves. But they, measuring themselves by themselves, and comparing themselves among themselves, are not wise. [13]We, however, will not boast beyond measure, but within the limits of the sphere which God appointed us—a sphere which especially includes you.

¹⁴For we are not overextending ourselves (as though our authority did not extend to you), for it was to you that we came with the gospel of Christ; ¹⁵not boasting of things beyond measure, that is, in other men's labors, but having hope, that as your faith is increased, we shall be greatly enlarged by you in our sphere, ¹⁶to preach the gospel in the regions beyond you, and not to boast in another man's sphere of accomplishment.

¹⁷But "he who glories, let him glory in the LORD." ¹⁸For not he who commends himself is approved, but whom the Lord commends.

EXPLORATION

1. What is the basic argument or conflict taking place in Corinth?

2. Paul asserts that, underneath the surface of things, the enemy (i.e., the devil) has a foothold in the church at Corinth. What does this mean, and how could such a thing happen?

3. How does Paul advocate dealing with wrong thinking and wrong behavior in the church?

4. Paul is not eager to confront the small group of Corinthians who continue to oppose his God-given authority, but he is willing to do whatever is necessary to preserve the church. Why is this kind of bold leadership important?

5. How should we be warned by this incident, in which believable suggestions were being made by seemingly spiritual people using lots of religious lingo?

INSPIRATION

Your heart is a fertile greenhouse ready to produce good fruit. Your mind is the doorway to your heart—the strategic place where you determine which seeds are sown and which seeds are discarded. The Holy Spirit is ready to help you manage and filter the thoughts that try to enter. He can help you guard your heart.

He stands with you on the threshold. A thought approaches, a questionable thought. Do you throw open the door and let it enter? Of course not. You *"fight to capture every thought until it acknowledges the authority of Christ"* (2 Cor. 10:5 PHILLIPS). You don't leave the door unguarded. You stand equipped with hand-cuffs and leg irons, ready to capture any thought not fit to enter.

For the sake of discussion, let's say a thought regarding your personal value approaches. With all the cockiness of a neighborhood bully, the thought swaggers up to the door and says, "You're a loser. All your life you've been a loser. You've blown relationships and jobs and ambitions. You might as well write the word *bum* on your resume, for that is what you are."

The ordinary person would throw open the door and let the thought in. Like a seed from a weed, it would find fertile soil and take root and bear thorns of inferiority. The average person would say, "You're right. I'm a bum. Come on in."

But as a Christian, you aren't your average person. You are led by the Spirit. So rather than let the thought in, you take it captive. You handcuff it and march it down the street to the courthouse where you present the thought before the judgment seat of Christ.

"Jesus, this thought says I'm a bum and a loser and that I'll never amount to any-thing. What do you think?"

See what you are doing? You are submitting the thought to the authority of Jesus. If Jesus agrees with the thought, then let it in. If not, kick it out. In this case Jesus disagrees.

How do you know if Jesus agrees or disagrees? You open your Bible. (From *Just Like Jesus* by Max Lucado)

REACTION

6. How would it change your life if you developed this discipline of arresting and examining every thought?

7. What can we learn here about the character and resolve of the enemy of our souls?

8. Why are Paul's ideas about how and what to think more valid than the ideas of the opposing religious leaders in Corinth?

9. What concrete steps can you take to submit every thought to the authority of Christ? (Hint: see Acts 17:10–12 for an example.)

10. Can you think of a time when wrong thinking resulted in wrong choices in your life? How about when right thinking led to wise choices?

11. What does this chapter suggest about the role of spiritual leaders in helping their followers think and live in ways that honor God?

LIFE LESSONS

The universe is not a neutral place. There is a war taking place, and the primary battleground is in our minds. All day every day we are bombarded with words, ideas, images, and suggestions. From advertisements to blogs, and from scientists to TV preachers, we face continual exposure to various perspectives and values. Not all of the information to which we are exposed is true. Much of it is unhealthy and opposed to what God says. And since ideas always have consequences, since what we believe ultimately does determine how we will behave, we must take radical action. What can we do? Wake up. Put on God's armor (Eph. 6). Pray for wisdom. Think critically. Practice discernment. Renew our minds daily (Rom. 12:2).

DEVOTION

Almighty God, prompt me this day to remember that I am in a spiritual battle. What I think and believe will affect the way I live. Grant me the insight to see the world as you see it. Help me to think like Jesus more and more so that I live like him more and more.

For more Bible passages on spiritual warfare, see Romans 13:12; 2 Corinthians 6:7; Ephesians 6:10–17; 1 Timothy 6:12; and 1 Peter 2:11; 5:8.

To complete the book of 2 Corinthians during this twelve-part study, read 2 Corinthians 10:1–18.

JOURNALING

Describe the current state of your heart and mind. What are the thoughts that create the most havoc in your soul?

LESSON TEN

PERSEVERANCE

MAX
LUCADO

REFLECTION

In Bible usage, the verb *persevere* literally means to "remain under." Much more than the common notion of passively resigning to life's difficulties, it suggests a courageous ability to bear hardships in a triumphant way. Given this meaning, who are your personal heroes of perseverance and why?

SITUATION

His leadership and authority challenged by certain unnamed rival preachers, Paul reluctantly spelled out a primary difference between him and them: If I'm not a genuine apostle, called by God, then why would I willingly endure so much for the gospel? And why are these self-proclaimed spiritual leaders so eager to avoid hardships?

OBSERVATION

Read 2 Corinthians 11:16–31 from the NCV or the NKJV.

NCV

16I tell you again: No one should think I am a fool. But if you think so, accept me as you would accept a fool. Then I can brag a little, too. 17When I brag because I feel sure of myself, I am not talking as the Lord would talk but as a fool. 18Many people are brag-ging about their lives in the world. So I will brag too. 19You are wise, so you will gladly be patient with fools! 20You are even patient with those who order you around, or use you, or trick you, or think they are better than you, or hit you in the face. 21It is shame-ful to me to say this, but we were too "weak" to do those things to you!

But if anyone else is brave enough to brag, then I also will be brave and brag. (I am talking as a fool.) 22Are they Hebrews? So am I. Are they Israelites? So am I. Are they from Abraham's family? So am I. 23Are they serving Christ? I am serving him more. (I am crazy to talk like this.) I have worked much harder than they. I have been in prison more often. I have been hurt more in beatings. I have been near death many times. 24Five times the Jews have given me their punishment of thirty-nine lashes with a whip. 25Three different times I was beaten with rods. One time I was almost stoned to death. Three times I was in ships that wrecked, and one of those times I spent a night and a day in the sea. 26I have gone on many travels and have been in danger from rivers, thieves, my own people, the Jews, and those who are not Jews. I have been in danger in cities, in places where no one lives, and on the sea. And I have been in danger with false Christians. 27I have done hard and tiring work, and many times I did not sleep. I have been hungry and thirsty, and many times I have been without food. I have been cold and without clothes. 28Besides all this, there is on me every day the load of my concern for all the churches. 29I feel weak every time someone is weak, and I feel upset every time someone is led into sin.

30If I must brag, I will brag about the things that show I am weak. 31God knows I am not lying. He is the God and Father of the Lord Jesus Christ, and he is to be praised forever.

NKJV

16I say again, let no one think me a fool. If otherwise, at least receive me as a fool, that I also may boast a little. 17What I speak, I speak not according to the Lord, but as it were, foolishly, in this confidence of boasting. 18Seeing that many boast according to the flesh, I also will boast. 19For you put up with fools gladly, since you yourselves are wise! 20For you put up with it if one brings you into bondage, if one devours you, if one takes from you, if one exalts himself, if one strikes you on the face. 21To our shame I say that we were too weak for that! But in whatever anyone is bold—I speak foolishly—I am bold also.

22Are they Hebrews? So am I. Are they Israelites? So am I. Are they the seed of Abraham? So am I. 23Are they ministers of Christ?—I speak as a fool—I am more: in labors more abundant, in stripes above measure, in prisons more frequently, in deaths often. 24From the Jews five times I received forty stripes minus one. 25Three times I was beaten with rods; once I was stoned; three times I was shipwrecked; a night and a day I have been in the deep; 26in journeys often, in perils of waters, in perils of robbers, in perils of my own countrymen, in perils of the Gentiles, in perils in the city, in perils in the wilderness, in perils in the sea, in perils among false brethren; 27in weariness and toil, in sleeplessness often, in hunger and thirst, in fastings often, in cold and nakedness— 28besides the other things, what comes upon me daily: my deep concern for all the churches. 29Who is weak, and I am not weak? Who is made to stumble, and I do not burn with indignation?

30If I must boast, I will boast in the things which concern my infirmity. 31The God and Father of our Lord Jesus Christ, who is blessed forever, knows that I am not lying.

EXPLORATION

1. When, if ever, is it legitimate for one Christian to compare his or her "spiritual résumé" to another's?

2. Proverbs 27:2 (NCV) says, "Don't praise yourself. Let someone else do it." How do we reconcile Paul's comments here with this ancient command?

3. What's more difficult and why—enduring physical hardship or emotional stress?

4. Why is perseverance such an important quality for Christian leaders?

5. Why does Paul choose to boast of things that showed his weakness?

INSPIRATION

One of God's cures for weak faith? A good, healthy struggle. Several years ago our family visited Colonial Williamsburg, a re-creation of eighteenth-century America in Williamsburg, VA. If you ever visit there, pay special attention to the work of the silversmith. The craftsman places an ingot of silver on an anvil and pounds it with a sledgehammer. Once the metal is flat enough for shaping, into the furnace it goes. The worker alternately heats and pounds the metal until it takes the shape of a tool he can use.

Heating, pounding. Heating, pounding.

Deadlines, traffic.

Arguments, disrespect.

Loud sirens, silent phones.

Heating, pounding. Heating, pounding.

Did you know that the *smith* in *silversmith* comes from the old English word *smite*? Silversmiths are accomplished smiters. So is God. Once the worker is satisfied with the form of his tool, he begins to planish and pumice it. Using smaller hammers and abrasive pads, he taps, rubs, and decorates. And no one stops him. No one yanks the hammer out of his hand and says, "Go easy on that silver. You've pounded enough!" No, the craftsman buffets the metal until he is finished with it. Some silversmiths, I'm told, keep polishing until they can see their face in the tool. When will God stop with you? When he sees his reflection in you. (From *Come Thirsty* by Max Lucado)

REACTION

6. What do you think of such an idea—that God not only allows, but actually participates in the painful shaping of his children?

7. What kinds of tough life situations are the most difficult for you to endure?

8. If critics attacked your character and faith, what "credentials" would you offer to show the genuineness of your Christian experience?

9. Do you agree with Paul's basic premise, that the unwillingness to endure suggests a lack of conviction—that perseverance is one of the defining marks of a believer? Why or why not?

10. How can we tell the difference between God-honoring perseverance and stubbornness or allegiance to a wrong-headed cause?

11. What have been the greatest hardships in your life, and what have you learned through them?

LIFE LESSONS

As imperfect people living among other flawed people in a fallen world, we should never be surprised when life is unpleasant. But even more than that, we should recall that our status as children of God means the evil one singles us out for special attack. We can respond to these realities by complaining and becoming bitter. Or we can decide, with divine help, through the indwelling power of the Spirit of God, to endure triumphantly. We can let the irritations and trials of life shape us into the people God created us to be. When we surrender to the inevitable process, determined to hang in there and glorify Christ no matter what, our character changes. And as it does we become powerful witnesses to the reality of God.

DEVOTION

Father, thank you for Paul's remarkable example—his rock-solid conviction of the reality of the gospel, that enabled him to endure all kinds of difficulties. Make me willing to pay any price and bear any burden for the hope of making you smile and the joy of making you known.

For more Bible passages on perseverance, see Romans 5:1–5; Hebrews 12:1; and James 1:2–8.

To complete the book of 2 Corinthians during this twelve-part study, read 2 Corinthians 11:1–33.

JOURNALING

The most trying situations in my life just now, the areas in which I need a second wind of perseverance are . . .

LESSON ELEVEN

SUSTAINING GRACE

MAX LUCADO

REFLECTION

When a person speaks of his spiritual *story* or his spiritual *journey*, he means his unique personal experience of responding to God's gracious involvement in his life. In your own spiritual life, when and where have you encountered God most vividly?

SITUATION

In an attempt to win back the confidence and support of a group of Corinthian Christians who question his spiritual credentials, Paul speaks candidly about all his experiences with God: certain sublime, ecstatic moments but mostly long stretches of struggle.

OBSERVATION

Read 2 Corinthians 12:1–13 from the NCV or the NKJV.

NCV

¹I must continue to brag. It will do no good, but I will talk now about visions and revelations from the Lord. ²I know a man in Christ who was taken up to the third heaven fourteen years ago. I do not know whether the man was in his body or out of his body, but God knows. ³⁻⁴And I know that this man was taken up to paradise. I don't know if he was in his body or away from his body, but God knows. He heard things he is not able to explain, things that no human is allowed to tell. ⁵I will brag about a man like that, but I will not brag about myself, except about my weaknesses. ⁶But if I wanted to brag about myself, I would not be a fool, because I would be telling the truth. But I will not brag about myself. I do not want people to think more of me than what they see me do or hear me say.

7So that I would not become too proud of the wonderful things that were shown to me, a painful physical problem was given to me. This problem was a messenger from Satan, sent to beat me and keep me from being too proud. 8I begged the Lord three times to take this problem away from me. 9But he said to me, "My grace is enough for you. When you are weak, my power is made perfect in you." So I am very happy to brag about my weaknesses. Then Christ's power can live in me. 10For this reason I am happy when I have weaknesses, insults, hard times, sufferings, and all kinds of troubles for Christ. Because when I am weak, then I am truly strong.

11I have been talking like a fool, but you made me do it. You are the ones who should say good things about me. I am worth nothing, but those "great apostles" are not worth any more than I am! 12When I was with you, I patiently did the things that prove I am an apostle—signs, wonders, and miracles. 13So you received everything that the other churches have received. Only one thing was different: I was not a burden to you. Forgive me for this!

NKJV

1It is doubtless not profitable for me to boast. I will come to visions and revelations of the Lord: 2I know a man in Christ who fourteen years ago—whether in the body I do not know, or whether out of the body I do not know, God knows—such a one was caught up to the third heaven. 3And I know such a man—whether in the body or out of the body I do not know, God knows— 4how he was caught up into Paradise and heard inexpressible words, which it is not lawful for a man to utter. 5Of such a one I will boast; yet of myself I will not boast, except in my infirmities. 6For though I might desire to boast, I will not be a fool; for I will speak the truth. But I refrain, lest anyone should think of me above what he sees me to be or hears from me.

7And lest I should be exalted above measure by the abundance of the revelations, a thorn in the flesh was given to me, a messenger of Satan to buffet me, lest I be exalted above measure. 8Concerning this thing I pleaded with the Lord three times that it might depart from me. 9And He said to me, "My grace is sufficient for you, for My strength is made perfect in weakness." Therefore most gladly I will rather boast in my infirmities, that the power of Christ may rest upon me. 10Therefore I take pleasure in infirmities, in reproaches, in needs, in persecutions, in distresses, for Christ's sake. For when I am weak, then I am strong.

11I have become a fool in boasting; you have compelled me. For I ought to have been commended by you; for in nothing was I behind the most eminent apostles, though I am nothing. 12Truly the signs of an apostle were accomplished among you with all per-severance, in signs and wonders and mighty deeds. 13For what is it in which you were inferior to other churches, except that I myself was not burdensome to you? Forgive me this wrong!

EXPLORATION

1. What exactly happened in this vision, and what conclusion does Paul want us to draw about it?

2. In describing his vision, why does Paul speak of himself in the third person?

3. What does Paul mean when he speaks of receiving a "thorn in the flesh"?

4. Why did Paul view this ongoing difficulty—whatever it was—as a good thing?

5. How is Paul's attitude different from common, everyday "positive thinking"?

INSPIRATION

You wonder why God doesn't remove temptation from your life? If he did, you might lean on your strength instead of his grace. A few stumbles might be what you need to convince you: His grace is sufficient for your sin.

You wonder why God doesn't remove the enemies in your life? Perhaps because he wants you to love like he loves. Anyone can love a friend, but only a few can love an enemy. So what if you aren't everyone's hero? His grace is sufficient for your self-image.

You wonder why God doesn't alter your personality? You, like Paul, are a bit rough around the edges? Say things you later regret or do things you later question? Why doesn't God make you more like him? He is. He's just not finished yet. Until he is, his grace is sufficient to overcome your flaws.

You wonder why God doesn't heal you? He *has* healed you. If you are in Christ, you have a perfected soul and a perfected body. His plan is to give you the soul now and the body when you get home. He may choose to heal parts of your body before heaven. But if he doesn't, don't you still have reason for gratitude? If he never gave you more than eternal life, could you ask for more than that? His grace is sufficient for gratitude.

Wonder why God won't give you a skill? If only God had made you a singer or a runner or a writer or a missionary. But there you are, tone-deaf, slow of foot and mind. Don't despair. God's grace is still sufficient to finish what he began. And until he's finished, let Paul remind you that the power is in the message, not the messenger. His grace is sufficient to speak clearly even when you don't.

For all we don't know about thorns, we can be sure of this. God would prefer we have an occasional limp than a perpetual strut. And if it takes a thorn for him to make his point, he loves us enough not to pluck it out.

God has every right to say no to us. We have every reason to say thanks to him. (From *In the Grip of Grace* by Max Lucado)

REACTION

6. What would be the likely response if we had the strength and knowledge to handle every situation?

7. Describe a recent situation in your life in which you found God's strength more than able to compensate for your personal inability.

8. How can you tell when you are becoming spiritually proud?

9. What are some of the ways God has humbled you?

10. How, practically speaking, can a Christian develop the quality of delighting in weakness and trusting more fully in the power of God?

11. Do you have a "thorn in the flesh" that God refuses to remove? If so, what is it and how have you been made stronger through it?

LIFE LESSONS

The Bible likens the Christian life to a lifelong walk or even a race (2 Tim. 4:7) down a narrow road (Matt. 7:14). In other places we find military metaphors (Eph. 6:10–17; 2 Tim. 2:3–4). Such stark imagery—life as both a dangerous journey and a vicious battle—should prompt us to stop and ponder. How can we keep going to the end? How do we emerge victorious? Paul's experience and counsel are helpful. God does not protect his beloved children from trials. Rather he helps us overcome them. Surprisingly, he works most effectively in and through our weaknesses. When we are clueless and powerless, we are much more likely to cry out to him and to cling to him. Whether times are good or bad, we live by grace. Always, we are called to rely fully on his amazing favor.

DEVOTION

How true it is, Lord . . . you do work and move in mysterious ways. Thank you for those moments when you are so near and real that I almost feel I can touch you. Thank you for the promise that in my darkest hours, you are with me and your grace is more than enough.

For more Bible passages on strength in weakness, see 1 Samuel 17; Isaiah 40:28–31; Romans 8:26; and 1 Corinthians 2:1–5.

To complete the book of 2 Corinthians during this twelve-part study, read 2 Corinthians 12:1–13.

JOURNALING

Where do you need to rely on God's grace and power in your life?

LESSON TWELVE

MATURITY

MAX
LUCADO

REFLECTION

In the same way that every infant needs to grow up, each spiritual newborn also needs to mature in his or her faith. Three related questions: What does it look like to grow spiritually? How can a person tell if he or she is growing? When have you grown the most dramatically in your faith journey?

SITUATION

Paul concludes his letter to the Corinthians with strong assurances of his love and with a heartfelt appeal for them to turn away from their worldly ways of thinking and living. The marks of a healthy, mature Christian community are purity, humility, and unity.

OBSERVATION

Read 2 Corinthians 12:19–13:11 from the NCV or the NKJV.

NCV

19Do you think we have been defending ourselves to you all this time? We have been speaking in Christ and before God. You are our dear friends, and everything we do is to make you stronger. 20I am afraid that when I come, you will not be what I want you to be, and I will not be what you want me to be. I am afraid that among you there may be arguing, jealousy, anger, selfish fighting, evil talk, gossip, pride, and confusion. 21I am afraid that when I come to you again, my God will make me ashamed before you. I may be saddened by many of those who have sinned because they have not changed their hearts or turned from their sexual sins and the shameful things they have done.

13:1I will come to you for the third time. "Every case must be proved by two or three witnesses." ²When I was with you the second time, I gave a warning to those who had sinned. Now I am away from you, and I give a warning to all the others. When I come to you again, I will not be easy with them. ³You want proof that Christ is speaking through me. My proof is that he is not weak among you, but he is powerful. ⁴It is true that he was weak when he was killed on the cross, but he lives now by God's power. It is true that we are weak in Christ, but for you we will be alive in Christ by God's power.

⁵Look closely at yourselves. Test yourselves to see if you are living in the faith. You know that Jesus Christ is in you—unless you fail the test. ⁶But I hope you will see that we ourselves have not failed the test. ⁷We pray to God that you will not do anything wrong. It is not important to see that we have passed the test, but it is important that you do what is right, even if it seems we have failed. ⁸We cannot do anything against the truth, but only for the truth. ⁹We are happy to be weak, if you are strong, and we pray that you will become complete. ¹⁰I am writing this while I am away from you so that when I come I will not have to be harsh in my use of authority. The Lord gave me this author-ity to build you up, not to tear you down.

¹¹Now, brothers and sisters, I say good-bye. Try to be complete. Do what I have asked you to do. Agree with each other, and live in peace. Then the God of love and peace will be with you.

NKJV

¹⁹Again, do you think that we excuse ourselves to you? We speak before God in Christ. But we do all things, beloved, for your edification. ²⁰For I fear lest, when I come, I shall not find you such as I wish, and that I shall be found by you such as you do not wish; lest there be contentions, jealousies, outbursts of wrath, selfish ambitions, backbitings, whisperings, conceits, tumults; ²¹lest, when I come again, my God will humble me among you, and I shall mourn for many who have sinned before and have not repented of the uncleanness, fornication, and lewdness which they have practiced.

¹³:¹This will be the third time I am coming to you. "By the mouth of two or three wit-nesses every word shall be established." ²I have told you before, and foretell as if I were present the second time, and now being absent I write to those who have sinned before, and to all the rest, that if I come again I will not spare— ³since you seek a proof of Christ speaking in me, who is not weak toward you, but mighty in you. ⁴For though He was crucified in weakness, yet He lives by the power of God. For we also are weak in Him, but we shall live with Him by the power of God toward you.

⁵Examine yourselves as to whether you are in the faith. Test yourselves. Do you not know yourselves, that Jesus Christ is in you?—unless indeed you are disqualified. ⁶But I trust that you will know that we are not disqualified.

⁷Now I pray to God that you do no evil, not that we should appear approved, but that you should do what is honorable, though we may seem disqualified. ⁸For we can do nothing against the truth, but for the truth. ⁹For we are glad when we are weak and you are strong. And this also we pray, that you may be made complete. ¹⁰Therefore I write these things being absent, lest being present I should use sharpness, according to the authority which the Lord has given me for edification and not for destruction.

¹¹Finally, brethren, farewell. Become complete. Be of good comfort, be of one mind, live in peace; and the God of love and peace will be with you.

EXPLORATION

1. Paul lists some negative behaviors that he fears are persistent among the Corinthians. How would his list differ if he were writing to your church or small group?

2. What does Paul mean by living "by the power of God" (13:4)?

3. What does it mean to *"examine yourselves as to whether you are in the faith"* (13:5 NKJV)?

4. Despite his stern words, Paul's desire was to build up the Corinthians, not tear them down (see 12:19; 13:10). What are some specific ways Christians can build up one another?

5. In closing, Paul pleads with his readers to *"agree with each other, and live in peace"* (v. 11 NCV). Why is this so much more easily said than done?

INSPIRATION

Suspicion and distrust often lurk at God's table. The Baptists distrust the Methodists. The Church of Christ avoids the Presbyterians. The Calvinists scoff at the Armenians. Charismatics. Immersionists. Patternists. Around the table the siblings squabble, and the Father sighs.

The Father sighs because he has a dream. *"I have other sheep that are not in this flock, and I must bring them also. They will listen to my voice, and there will be one flock and one shepherd"* (John 10:16 NCV).

God has only one flock. Somehow we missed that. Religious division is not his idea. Franchises and sectarianism are not in God's plan. God has one flock. The flock has one shepherd. And though we may think there are many, we are wrong. There is only one.

Never in the Bible are we told to create unity. We are simply told to maintain the unity that exists. Paul exhorts us to preserve *"the unity which the Spirit gives"* (Eph. 4:3 NEB). Our task is not to invent unity, but to acknowledge it . . .

By the way, the church names we banter about? They do not exist in heaven. The Book of Life does not list your denomination next to your name. Why? Because it is not the denomination that saves you. And I wonder, if there are no denominations in heaven, why do we have denominations on earth?

What would happen (I know this is a crazy thought), but what would happen if all the churches agreed, on a given day, to change their names to simply "church"? What if any reference to any denomination were removed and we were all just Christians? And then when people chose which church to attend, they wouldn't do so by the sign outside . . . they'd do so by the hearts of the people inside. And then when people were asked what church they attended, their answer wouldn't be a label but just a location.

And then we Christians wouldn't be known for what divides us; instead we'd be

known for what unites us—our common Father.

Crazy idea? Perhaps.

But I think God would like it. It was his to begin with. (From *A Gentle Thunder* by Max Lucado)

REACTION

6. How—like Paul—can we develop the courageous willingness to speak frankly but lovingly to others about the importance of growing spiritually?

7. Is it a common practice for you to take spiritual inventory? How, and how often, should one do such a thing?

8. What people in your life need to be built up today, and in what ways?

9. What does it mean, in practical terms, to "become complete" (13:11 NKJV)?

10. Do you currently have relationships with other believers marked by friction and discord? What is God urging you to do?

11. As you think back over your study of 2 Corinthians, what primary lessons or principles have meant the most to you and why?

LIFE LESSONS

It is the nature of healthy organisms to grow. The failure of a living thing to mature and thrive is not normal. A child who develops slowly, or not at all, is the cause of great concern. Appointments are made. Specialists are consulted. Tests are conducted. In the same way, those who know Christ should be developing spiritually. There should be some signs of growth and change. When we claim to be followers of Christ, but we do not exhibit the conduct and character of Christ, something is clearly wrong. Examine your own life. Do you have a desire for personal purity? Are you marked by a growing humility? Do you pursue unity with other believers? These are reliable indicators of divine transformation.

DEVOTION

Father, I am reminded again that not growing is not an option for your children. You have begun a good work in me that will continue until Christ comes again. Make me a willing partner in this great eternal makeover. Thank you for your patience when I stumble.

For more Bible passages on maturity, see 1 Corinthians 3:1–4; Ephesians 4:14–15; Hebrews 6:1; 1 Peter 2:2.

To complete the book of 2 Corinthians during this twelve-part study, read 2 Corinthians 12:14–13:14.

JOURNALING

Describe two or three areas of your life in which you'd like to see God help you mature.